YOUR KNOWLEDGE

- We will publish your bachelor's and master's thesis, essays and papers

- Your own eBook and book - sold worldwide in all relevant shops

- Earn money with each sale

Upload your text at www.GRIN.com and publish for free

Bibliographic information published by the German National Library:

The German National Library lists this publication in the National Bibliography; detailed bibliographic data are available on the Internet at http://dnb.dnb.de .

Imprint:

Copyright © 2015 GRIN Verlag, Open Publishing GmbH
Print and binding: Books on Demand GmbH, Norderstedt Germany
ISBN: 9783668262843

This book at GRIN:

http://www.grin.com/en/e-book/336692/racism-and-stereo-types-in-walt-disney-movies-an-analysis-of-pocahontas

GRIN - Your knowledge has value

Since its foundation in 1998, GRIN has specialized in publishing academic texts by students, college teachers and other academics as e-book and printed book. The website www.grin.com is an ideal platform for presenting term papers, final papers, scientific essays, dissertations and specialist books.

Visit us on the internet:

http://www.grin.com/

http://www.facebook.com/grincom

http://www.twitter.com/grin_com

Anonym

Racism and stereo types in Walt Disney movies. An analysis of "Pocahontas" (1995)

GRIN Publishing

Racism and stereo types in Walt Disney movies –
An analysis of Pocahontas (1995)

Table of Contents

1. Introduction 1

2. Theoretical Concepts 3

    2.1   Race 3

    2.2   Racism 4

       2.2.1.   The history of Racism – a summary 5

    2.3   Othering 7

    2.4   Stereo Types 8

       2.4.1.   The Stereotype Content Model by Fiske et al. 2002 9

3. Disney's Pocahontas – A short summary 11

4. Pocahontas' real life 12

5. Differences between the real and the fictive story 15

6. Racism and Stereotypes in Pocohontas (1995) 16

7. Conclusion 20

8. Reference list 21

9. Appendix I

1. Introduction

In our globalized world, the mixing of cultures, languages and traditions has been playing a central role in today's societies. One unpleasant side effect, however, is the occurrence of racial thoughts among people. Some people think that they are more worth than others and feel superior towards them, for example, due to their skin color or religion. The phenomenon of racism can not only be seen in its strongest form in Germany during the Nazi Regime or in South Africa during the apartheid regime, but also, for instance, today in the United States, where unarmed black people got killed by white policemen.

Furthermore, there can be seen racist elements in films, not only for adults but also for children. In 1995 Ron Disney published the movie Pocahontas, which deals with the first English settlements in the New World North America. Describing the first meeting of white English settlers and Native American tribe members, it tells the love story of Princess Pocahontas, the daughter of Chief Powhatan, who falls in love with the Captain John Smith, a white English settler.

The aim of this paper is to analyze whether there can be found racist or stereotypical elements in Disney's movie Pocahontas. To start with, basic theoretical concepts will be introduced. The subchapter 2.1. focuses on the definition of race. Since the goal of this work is to find out whether there are racist elements in Pocahontas, it is necessary to define race. It will become clear that race is a constructed characterization of people and that it is not a biologically inherent, but created in the people's minds. This will form the basis for the next subchapter 2.2. which deals with the concept of racism. It will be emphasized that the concept of racism is severe complex and can have different definitions due to personal appraisals. Furthermore, it will be pointed out that racism as well is a constructed phenomenon which does not arise because of characteristic features but because of social and cultural structures.

The following part of the paper sets its focus on the summarized historical development of racism. It will be outlined that there had been many racist actions before the actual name of this phenomenon "racism" was introduced in the 1930s. Starting already in antiquity among Greek and Romans who had slaves, racism went through the whole world story: Above all Jewish people as well as black people have been targets of the attacks. Whereas Jews were treated badly because of their different, non-Christian religion, black people were considered to be evil because of their dark skin color. Its peak reached racism during the Nazi time in Germany where the dictator Adolf Hitler tried to exterminate a whole ethnical group and during the apartheid in South Africa where the purity of the race was considered to be so important that sexual relations between white and black people were forbidden.

After that, the concept of Othering and Otherness will be shortly introduced. It will be explained that one in-group feels superior to one or more out-groups by finding real or imagined differences. It is unavoidable to define this concept because Disney movie's male protagonist Captain John Smith clearly differentiates himself and his culture from the Native American Pocahontas'.

Furthermore, the concept of stereotypes will be introduced. Sundquist (1987) defines stereotypes as "fixed or general pattern and lacks individual distinguishing marks or qualities". The chapter will present the three dimensions of stereotypes which are firstly that stereotypes are aids to explanation, secondly that stereotypes are energy-saving devices and thirdly that stereotypes are shared group beliefs, according to McGarty, Yzerbyt and Spears (2002). The subchapter 2.3.1. focuses on the Stereotype Content Model by Fiske et al. 2002, which categorizes people into two dimensions, by analyzing and describing the influence of different social structural aspects on stereotypes.

The second part of the paper will deal with the content and the language of the movie Pocahontas. Chapter four will briefly summarize the plot of the Disney movie, whereas the following fifth chapter presents the real story of the Native American Matoaka, later called Pocahontas, on which the plot of the film is based. Since historians are still unclear about her existence, the chapter describes how Pocahontas live might have looked like before she met Captain John Smith. It is argued that due to the fact that when the 28-year-old Smith met Pocahontas, she must have been between ten and eleven years old and therefore not yet considered to be a woman. Consequently, it is doubted whether the two really had a romantic relationship and whether Pocahontas' famous rescue actually happened. Since there can be several differences between the real story of Pocahontas and the plot of Disney's movie, chapter six will be a comparison.

The chapter before last will put the emphasis on the movie itself. The result of the paper will be that racist and stereotypical element can be primarily seen in the language, the English figures, above all Captain John Smith and Governor Ratcliff, use. From the beginning they use the word savages to refer to the Native Americans and call it fun to exterminate the ethnic group. Furthermore, the lyrics of Ratcliff's song "Savages, savages" will be analyzed and it will be outlined how racist his language is towards the Indians.

The closing conclusion will summarize the most important facts and it will be outlined again that there can be stereotypical and racist features in the movie Pocahontas.

2. Theoretical Concepts

In the following chapter, the main theoretical concepts of racism will be introduced, in order to be able to apply them to the chosen examples of the Disney movie Pocahontas.

The following part will initially define the term race to afterwards go on with the term racism. Hereby, the focus will be on the definition of racism and a summary of its historical development. Furthermore, the concept of Othering, stereotypes as well as the Stereotype Content Model by Fiske et al. 2002 will be presented and defined.

2.1 Race

To define *racism* it is initially inevitable to clarify what *race* is. King and Stansfield (1990) define in their dictionary of genetics race as:

> A phenotypically and/or geographically distinctive subspecific group, composed of individuals inhabiting a defined geographical and/or ecological region, and possessing characteristic phenotypic and gene frequencies that distinguish it from other such groups. The number of racial groups that one wishes to recognize within a species is usually arbitrary but suitable for the purposes under investigation. (ibid, cited from Pigliucci, M. & J. Kaplany 2003: 1162).

That means that shared characteristics of a group are used to categorize people. In 1775, the German professor of medicine Johann Friedrich Blumenbach (1752 – 1840) published his doctoral dissertation "On the Natural Variety of Mankind" where he introduced a race-based classification. Rewriting it and publishing a second edition, Blumenbach changed the originally introduced four race groups, categorized geographically, to a five-race arrangement. The five races Blumenbach introduces are: Caucasian, the white race; Mongolian, the yellow race; Malayan, the tawny-colored race; Ethiopian, the black race; and American, the copper-colored race. Although the author argued to have chosen geographically features, it becomes clear that there was a shift to physical appearance (cf. Blumenbach 1795, cited from Bernasconi, R. & T. L. Lott 2000: 5ff.)

According to Rogers, D. & M. Bowman (2003), however, race is not a biologically valid classification but

> [...] a false classification of people that is not based on any real or accurate biological or scientific truth. In other words, the distinction we make between races, has nothing to do with scientific truth. Race is a political construction. A political construction is something created by people; that is not a natural development; is constructed or created for a political purpose. The concept of race was created as a classification of human beings with the purpose of giving power to white people and to legitimize the dominance of white people over non-white people. (ibid., p. 2).

The authors state that the concept of race was created by the people and used for political purposes. Furthermore, they claim that it was constructed to give power to the white people to be more powerful than non-white people.

2.2 Racism

In times of migration, "the movement of people from one place in the world to another for the purpose of taking up permanent or semipermanent residence, usually across a political boundary (von Abele 2005: 1), multiculturalism is a present phenomenon. Some people see this mixing of cultures as a possibility to grow personally, take it a joyful sign of mutual acceptance and as a rich endeavor (cf. Essed & Helwig 1992; Arredondo 1996, Hollands 1998, cited from Essed 2000:43). Others, however, see it as a source of hostility, prejudice and discrimination, mostly felt by Europeans who find the immigrants to be different (cf. Rattansi & Westwood 1994, cited from Essed 2002: 43). This negative feeling is called racism.

Fredrickson (2002), however, states that the general definition of Racism as "the hostile or negative feeling of one ethnic group or 'people' toward another and the actions resulting from such attitudes" is often used too loosely and unreflectively (cf. ibid, p. 1). According to the author, these feelings of antipathy are sometimes very brutal and enduring like in the case of the German dictator Adolf Hitler so that this definition seems to be too weak (cf. ibid.).

According to Blommaert & Verschueren (1994) racism can stand for different personal definitions: Neo-nazis and the extreme right equal racism for some people, whereas other people would say that racism is the institutional discrimination through practices, laws and customs that underline racial and ethnical differences and inequalities. A third person might say that racism is a personal prejudice (cf. ibid, cited from Essed 2002: 43), "an antipathy based on a faulty and inflexible generalization" (Allport 1954, cited from Bodenhausen, G. V. & J. A. Richeson 2010: 342).

Van Dijk (1991; 1993) and Feagin & Feagin (1993) claim that racism is a problem which was created by human beings and is therefore not inherent to a person's character. Consequently, it is no personal characteristic, but a social and cultural phenomenon, which leads to exclusion and inferiority of minority groups (cf. ibid, cited from Essed 2002: 43).

4

2.2.1.   The history of Racism – a summary

According to Fredrickson (2002), the term *racism* was used commonly for the first time in the 1930s, to describe the phenomenon of Nazis' theories to persecute Jewish people. Nevertheless, the phenomenon itself existed before Adolf Hitler had seized power and therefore before the term *racism* was introduced (cf. ibid, p. 5).

Already the Greeks distinguished between civilized and barbarous people. Civilized people lived in city-states and took part in the political life. Barbarous people, however, lived under rustic living conditions and were ruled (cf. Hannaford 1996, cited from Fredrickson 2002: 17). Also the Romans had slaves from all nationalities and skin colors that could be found around their empire's frontiers. Furthermore, there has been ethnic prejudice in antiquity as well. From the beginning, Christians had an anti-Jewish attitude, although Christianity arose from Judaism. Jews who had not converted to the Christian religion, were considered to be criminal and guilty for human crimes (Poliakov 1965, cited from Fredrickson 2002: 18).

In the twelfth and thirteens century, Jews were confronted with even more hostile attitudes of the European Christians. They often worked as international merchants and traders, but within the time, through the commercial competition Christians forced them to make them lend money at interest, which was considered to be unpopular and sinful. This found its climax in violent massacres of the Jewish people leading to the assumption by the thirteenth and fourteenth century that the Jews even were demons and in contact with the devil. During the Black Death in the mid-fourteenth century, when 1.5 million people out of around 4 million people were killed, Jewish people were killed, because it was thought that they had poisoned the wells and therefore killed many Christians (cf. ibid, p. 19ff.).

In the middle ages, when Catholic Europe expanded throughout the entire world, the racist thoughts expanded as well. According to the historian Robert Bartlett, attitudes of superiority and dominance towards other people were taken to new lands and displayed towards indigenous people (cf. ibid, p. 23).

During the fifteenth century, Europeans started to have contact with sub-Saharan Africans. These "exotic" people were considered to be horrifying and monstrous, since devils and the executioners of martyrs were often portrayed as black creatures, but also seen as heroes and saints, since the first non-Jewish person who converted to the Christian religion was an Ethiopian eunuch (cf. ibid, p. 26f.). Winthrop (1968) and Devisse (1979) claim that since the black has a symbolic association of being evil and death and white is associated with purity and goodness, had an influence on the people's mind, tending to see light-skinned people of higher value than people with dark skin (cf. ibid, cited from Fredrickson 2002: 26f.).

Within the fifteenth century, the partly positive attitude towards people with black skin disappeared. During this time, European countries started to have African slaves instead of other European slaves, which shows their supremacist feelings. Being treated as instruments of production, non-Christian black slaves were assumed to be easier ruled and there was the chance to convert them (Adas 1998, cited from Fredrickson 2002: 30f.).

When the Spanish encountered the New World, they considered the Native Americans to be a "monstrous race" or "wild men". Also Columbus called the Indians he met on islands "cannibals" who have to be exterminated or subdued by force (cf. ibid, p. 36). Even after the Native Americans were baptized, the cultural discrimination against them on part of the Spanish continued and could also be seen in peninsular Spain, where people who were not considered to be real Spanish were excluded, called *limpieza del sangre* which equals cleanliness of blood (cf. ibid, p. 40f.).

Holding black slaves persisted until the nineteenth century and therefore, the assumption that they were inferior and servile continued to be stuck into the people's minds. In late-seventeenth-century, the American state of Virginia established a serious of laws which stated that Black slaves who converted to the Christian religion were still not free, which led to the fact that there were still racist attitudes towards them (cf. ibid, p.45).

Whereas the origins of racism can be found primarily in religious contexts, the nineteenths century was characterized by emancipation, nationalism, and imperialism. Above all the growth of nationalism played a big role in Germany, where a culture-coded variant of racism arose. The disapproval of the Germans was directed the Jewish people who were not "true German". The climax of German racism came in in the twentieth century during Hitler's Nazi Regime who tried to exterminate a whole ethnic group due to his racist ideologies (cf. Fredrickson 2003).

In addition, the American south passed racial segregation laws which prohibited black people to vote. Black men, who were portrayed as beats watching after white women and other racial propaganda led to terrible procedures such as lynching. Furthermore, it was aimed to prevent intercultural marriages because of the fear of sexual contamination. It took until the 1960s when the Civil Right Movement ended the racial segregation and discrimination with the help of international support (cf. ibid.).

In South Africa, however, the racial attitudes against black people continued until the 1990s. Here again, the idea of the purity of the white race led to the fact that sexual relationships with black or colored people were forbidden. The "apartheid regime" ended in 1994, when the black freedom fighter Nelson Mandela became president (cf. ibid.).

Nonetheless, racism does not have to be on state level or determined by law, as shown in the examples before. There can also be individual racism or by institutions. Still today, racism can be seen all over the world. If one takes a look to the United States of America, for example, just recently on August 15th in 2015, the nineteen-year-old Afro-American unarmed student Christian Taylor was shot down by the white policeman Brad Miller. Only about one year ago, on August 9th in 2014, there happened a similar incident in Ferguson, Missouri, USA, where the African American Michael Brown was shot by the white policeman Darren Wilson. This activated a severe discussion about racism and equal rights in the United States and created a strong international stir (cf. Boren 2015).

Unfortunately, it is likely that racism will always play a role in societies. Regardless of the heritage of the population, we can find racism in all parts of the world, for example Germany, the United States or Spain.

2.3 Othering

I understand now that nothing but "otherness" killed Jews, and it began with naming them, by reducing them to the other. Then everything became possible. Even the worst atrocities like concentration camps or the slaughtering of civilians in Croatia or Bosnia. (Drakulić 1992, cited from Brons 2015: 69).

The term Othering refers to the creation of Otherness, meaning that a dominant in-group ("Us") constructs one or more out-groups ("Them" or "Others") which are dominated. This is due to the fact that the in-group stigmatizes existing or even imagined differences of the out-group/s. Consequently, the in-group constructs the others due to the fact that it gives itself an identity and sets itself apart. The out-group, however, has no identity based on simplifying and stigmatized stereotypes and is only coherent since it is put in opposition to the in-group (cf. Staszak 2008: 2).

The example of sex and gender can be taken as a good explanation. Whereas sex is a biological attribute which makes a difference between men and women, gender is constructed and not inherent, therefore it is Otherness (cf. ibid.).

2.4 Stereo Types

According to Sundquist (1987), the term "stereotype" was firstly used in the field of typography during the procedure of printing books, where it described printing plates which enabled to maintain the same printing surface for a long period. Within the course of time, its adjective stereotyped required the meaning of being repeated mechanically or being produced variationless. Today, a stereotype refers to "fixed or general pattern and lacks individual distinguishing marks or qualities" (cf. ibid., p. 19). Furthermore, stereo types are "simple rather than complex and differentiated" (Harding 1986, cited from Sundquist 1987: 19).

The American writer, reporter, and political commentator Walter Lippmann was the first one who wrote about the concept of stereotypes in social sciences in his book "public Opinion" from 1922. For him, stereotypes have two functions: the first one is that they facilitate our lives and the process of understanding people, because we can find categories that are shared by many people. The second function of stereotypes is that they lead to distortion, prejudices and falsification (Lippmann 1944, cited from Sundquist 1987:19). To go more in detail, McGarty, Yzerbyt and Spears (2002) state that if one wants to understand what stereotypes are, one has to consider three principles:

The first one says that stereotypes are aids to explanation, which means that they should help the perceiving person to understand a situation. Hereby, categorization plays an important role because it helps the person to find differences and similarities between people (cf. ibid, p. 2f.).

The second principle declares that stereotypes are energy-saving devices, meaning that they reduce the perceiver's effort. It is easier to put people in categories, ignoring their individual details. McGarty 1999 states that people do only have a limited capacity to use and process information. However, the surrounding world is full of information and therefore these information need a lot of capacity to be processed. As a result there is an overload of information and the people start to take over wrong perceptions of the world, take shorter ways and develop biases, which can be for example stereotypes. One can clearly see the negative aspect of this principle, which leads more to misunderstanding that to understanding (cf. McGarty 1999, cited from McGarty, Yzerbyt and Spears 2002: 3ff.).

Thirdly, stereotypes are shared group beliefs, so they should be part of the perceiver's widely accepted views and norms. Stereotypes do only perceive attention when they are shared by many people. Those shared stereotypes help to understand and to predict people's behavior of a certain group. Shared stereotypes arise from same thoughts and identical mental processes of the individuals. Some researchers say that these coincidental thoughts come from a shared environment, which leads to the same stereotypes. Others, however, say that people share culture, ideologies, social representation and a common cultural pool of knowledge, which leads to the same stereotypes In addition to that, there is a third supposition that shared stereotypes are normative beliefs. According to the authors, shared stereotypes do not only exist because people make same experiences or have the same knowledge, but because people coordinate their actions and behavior with each other. Members of the group participate want to be distinctive from other groups (cf. ibid, p. 5f.).

Moreover, the content of stereotypes can be influence by social structure. Discrimination and stereotypes interact, inasmuch as both can promote each other: Stereotypes can be a consequence of discrimination through justifying differences and disparities. On the other hand, stereotypes lead to discrimination due to influencing and changing opinions and beliefs. According to Hoffmann & Hurst (1990) and Eagly & Diekman (2005), the social role of a person represents his or her characteristics (cf. ibib, cited from Dovidio, J. F., Hewstone, M., Glick, P. & V. M. Esses 2010, p. 7). Therefore, members of a group with a high status are considered to have more motivation and more competence in contradistinction to groups with a lower social status (cf. ibid).

2.4.1.   The Stereotype Content Model by Fiske et al. 2002

The American researchers Fiske et al. introduced a Stereotype Content Model which analyzes and describes the influence of different social structural aspects on stereotypes. The model proposes two dimensions, namely the dimension of *warmth* and the dimension of *competence*.

Warmth is associated with cooperative, friendly, trustworthy, or helpful groups, whereas the dimension of *competence* hints at the high or low status of a group, and is therefore connected to efficiency, skills, intelligence and conscientiousness. According to Fiske et al. these two dimensions lead to stereotypes about social groups that can be categorized in four different quadrants:

The first quadrant is the competent, warm quadrant like in-groups, middle-class Americans, close allies or Christians for example. Housewives, elderly and disabled people, for instance, belong to the warm, but incompetent quadrant. The third quadrant, the cold and competent quadrant, contains for example Asians, Jews and rich people, whereas the incompetent, cold quadrant refers to derogated social groups, e.g. poor people, welfare recipients, who, according to the model, generate anger, and resentment (cf. Kervyn, N., Fiske, S. T. & V. Y. Yzerbyt 2013: 673f.; McGarty, Yzerbyt and Spears 2002: 7).

Furthermore, Bonacich (1973) and Hewstone &Ward (1985) state that this model could give an explanation for the fact that two distinct ethnic groups such as the Jews and the Chinese in e.g. Malaysia have been stereotyped in a similar way, since they both belong to the cold, but competent quadrant (cf. ibib, cited from McGarty, Yzerbyt and Spears 2002: 8).

However, there are also groups with moderate results in the two dimensions of *warmth* and *competence*, which cannot be categorized to one of the four quadrants. According to Fiske et al. (2002) Native Americans like Pocahontas as well as African Americans belong to this fifth cluster. Whereas African Americans were valued higher in the competence dimension than in the warmth dimension, and Asian Americans received an even higher valuation in competence, Native Americans judged with no significant difference between the two dimensions (cf. ibib, cited from Erhart 2013: 10). Erhart (2013) carried out a study with 58 undergraduate students at Arizona State University, 44 women and 14 men. Their task was to choose from a list of 145 adjectives the best-matching ten that they consider to be associated with cultural stereotypes of Native Americans. As a result the three most frequently selected adjectives were spiritual with forty-nine, brave with forty-five and family oriented with thirty-seven counts. But there were also adjectives chosen that reflected a low degree of competence, namely gambling with twenty-nine and alcoholic with twenty-seven counts (cf. ibid, p. 14; 18; 24).

To sum it up, the set of qualities that people think represent a certain group, is called stereotype. Therefore, stereotypes refer to beliefs and associations, people have about the character and attributes of other people. They influence the way people think about, process information about and react towards a group (cf. Dovidio, J. F., Hewstone, M., Glick, P. & V. M. Esses 2010, p. 8).

Before I will outline the different stereotypes and racist aspects in the Disney movie Pocahontas, I will initially introduce the Pocahontas' real life which is regarded as the basis of the movie. Following, I will give a short summary of the Disney movie Pocahontas from 1995.

3. Disney's Pocahontas – A short summary

In 1995, Ron Disney published a movie called "Pocahontas". Based on a true story, the movie is about a Native American princess, called Pocahontas. The movie was set in the New American World, when British settlers of the Virginia Company arrived in Jamestown, Virginia in 1607. One of the settlers is John Smith, whose voyage's leader Govenor Ratcliffe hopes to find gold in the New World. Their ship the "Susan Costant" gets caught in a storm and John has to rescue his crewmember Tom.

In the meantime, Pocahontas who is a young, beautiful, free spirited woman and the daughter of Chief Powhatan, is afraid of being married to a brave warrior of her tribe called Kocoum, who according to her is too serious for her personality. To find help, Pocahontas and her friends, a raccoon Meeko and hummingbird Flit, she visits the spiritual willow tree Grandmother Willow and talks to her about her undefinable dream about a spinning arrow. Hearing a noise, she climbs up the tree and sees that the British settlers were about to arrive.

When the settlers arrive, Governor Ratcliff immediately orders his crew to start looking for gold. John Smith, however, wants to explore the wilderness and meets Pocahontas. Although the chief's daughter was forbidden to have contact with the English since Kocoum got involved in a fight with some warriors, Pocahontas and John Smith are interested in each other and fall in love, promising to bring peace between the indigenous population and the English men. As a true sign of trust, Pocahontas introduces John to Grandmother Willow forgetting about their surroundings. Her friend Nakoma sees them together and warns Pocahontas' chosen future husband Kocoum. When John and Pocahontas meet again later, Kocoum and John's crewmember Tom observe them kissing. Filled with jealous feelings, Kocoum tries to kill John but Thomas shoots him dead. To save Tom from danger, John orders him to leave the place right before Pocahontas's tribesmen capture him. Powhatan, Pocahontas' father, proclaims war on the English and wants to start with executing John at sunrise.

Meanwhile, Tom warns his crewmen and tells them about John's demanded execution. Ratcliffe however, is more interested in gold than in the tribe and commands his men to fight against the tribe to exterminate it. Pocahontas, who feels guilty because Kocoum was killed, runs for Grandmother Willow's help. There, her friend Meeko hands her John Smith's compass, realizing the spinning arrow of her dream showing her the right way. Just in time, she reaches John, throws herself between him and her father, convincing Powhatan to stop the fight between the two groups. However, Ratcliff tries to shoot the chief, but instead hits John. His crewmember capture the Governor, whereas John needs to go back to England to be cured. He asks Pocahontas to come with him, but she chooses to stay with her tribe.

11

4. Pocahontas' real life

The story of Pocahontas is controversial, because still today historians are still unclear about her existence. At the end of the sixteenth century, around 1595, an American Indian girl named Matoaka would have been born in what the English called Virginia. Named Pocahontas in her childhood, meaning "little wanton" since she would have been very lively, would have loved to play and would have been hard to control, she would have been born as a daughter of the ruler of the land Powhatan (cf. Morenus). Being one of dozens children of Powhatan, Motoaka and her mother would have been sent back to her people after giving birth, since the many wives would have been only allowed to stay with the ruler of the land until they gave birth to his children. After eight to ten years, when the children would have been old enough to work and to support the people, they would have been allowed to come to their father's capital. Also Motoaka could have joined her father's household and probably would have done traditional women's work such as cooking, cleaning, collecting wild fruits and fire wood. During this time she would have been named Pocahontas, likely because her father Powhatan may have been thrilled by his daughter's wild character and therefore she would have become his favorite daughter by 1607 (cf. Rountree: Early Years), "the apple of his eye" (Morenus) (cf. Picture 1 of Appendix, p. I, to see imaginative picture of Pocahontas).

Pocahontas is probably most famous for saving John Smith and rescuing his life (cf. Picture 5 of Appendix, p. III to see picture of Captain John Smith). In 1607, the English man John Smith was captured by Powhatan's brother Opechancanough and finally came as an honored guest to Powhatan's capital. He was fed and interviewed by the ruler of the land, since he wanted to know why the English had come. It is likely that John Smith did not see Pocahontas, being about eleven years old at that time, at all, because she would have been needed to prepare the food and clean afterwards. Therefore, the following description by John Smith, which became legend and describes him being threatened with death and saved by Pocahontas, (cf. Picture 2 of appendix, p. I, to an imaginary picture of Pocahontas rescuing John Smith) could be false (cf. Rountree: John Smith):

> Two great stones were brought before Powhatan: then as many as could laid hands on him, dragged him to them, and thereon laid his head, and being ready with their clubs, to beate out his braines, Pocahontas the King's dearest daughter, when no intreaty could prevaile, got his head in her armes, and laid her owne upon his to save him from death: whereat the Emperour was contented he should live to make him hatchets, and her bells, beads, and copper [...] (Captain John Smith 1624, quoted from Morenus)

There have been many discussions about whether Pocahontas' protection really happened or not. It is argued that Smith might have never been in danger because the situation might have been an elaborate adoption ceremony (cf. Stebbins 2010).

Powhatan helped the English settlers by sending food to them via envoys, who were usually accompanied by Pocahontas. She helped the settlers to survive the winter by showing them how to define edible plants and teaching the indigenous language to John Smith. Within the time however, the relationship between the English men in the Jamestown colony and the ruler of the land Powhatan became difficult and critical. A strong drought and Powhatan's procedure to stop trading with the English made the settlers start burning down Native American villages, finally ending in the First Anglo-Powhatan War in 1608. To protect his people, Pocahontas' father moved his capital to another place far away from the settlers, and Pocahontas was not allowed to see John Smith and Jamestown anymore (cf. ibid.).

In 1609, Smith had to return to England because of a gunpowder wound and Pocahontas was informed that he died on his way back. Therefore, she left off visiting the settlers in Jamestown and in 1610, Pocahontas married Kocoum, who likely was a member of a tribe and a protector of her father. Three years later, the English Captain Samuel Argall came to Jamestown, knowing that there was no strong relationship between the settlers and the Native American tribes. When he discovered Pocahontas, he decided to kidnap her. He talked to the chief's brother Iopassus, who finally agreed to help him. Together with his wife, he lured Pocahontas to see Argall's ship and went onboard together. There, the English gave them food and on the next morning, Iopassus and his wife were allowed to leave the boat, whereas Pocahontas was kept, explaining she would have to stay since she was the ransom for English prisoners and weapons. Her father agreed because he hoped to open negotiations (cf. ibid).

Being kept in Jamestown, Pocahontas had to learn the English language, traditions and to take over the religion. During her religious instruction, she met John Rolfe, they fell in love and married in 1614 (cf. Mossiker 1976: 176) (cf. Picture 3 of the Appendix, p. II to see a picture of the marriage). In the same year, she converted to Christianity, was baptized "Rebecca", now Lady Rebecca Rolfe (cf. Picture 4 of Appendix, p. III) and soon gave birth to their son Thomas. The Virginia Company of London, who financed the settlement in Jamestown, started to see Pocahontas/Rebecca as an opportunity to become more interesting to Virginia, since she was a converted Christian who married an English man (cf. Pictures 5 & 6 of Appendix, p. IIIf. to see British Pocahontas/Rebecca). Furthermore, they sponsored her a travel to England where she met important people like Queen Anne and King James I. However, John Smith had not forgotten about his friend Pocahontas and visited her after a couple of months. Pocahontas was very angry about his behavior towards her fellowmen and made him aware of how nicely her father had treated the settlers (cf. Stebbins 2010.).

Three years later, in March 1617, Pocahontas/Rebecca, her husband John Rolfe and her son Thomas strived to return to Virginia, but she was too ill and had to stay in England. Shortly after, Pocahontas/Rebecca died of an unspecified illness. She was only twenty-one years old and was buried in England in 1617. Her husband returned to Virginia and let his son alone with relatives in England. Only about one year later, her beloved father Powhatan, the ruler of the land, died (cf. ibid.).

5. Differences between the real and the fictive story

If we compare the real story of Pocahontas and the Disney movie from Roy Disney in 1995, there can be found several similarities. According to Morenus, the movie depicts accurately the spirit the Native Americans and above all Pocahontas had and the situation in Jamestown, Virginia. Furthermore, the settings and the places are authentic, since James Ford and Powhatan were existing spots where Pocahontas probably lived. Also the surrounding such as the Virginian wilderness are portrayed in detail and the name of the ship *Susan Constant* is also true. Moreover, the author states that John Smith's crew was indeed led by a person called John Ratcliff and that John Smith himself wrote that Pocahontas saved his life, insulating him from her father (cf. ibid.).

Nevertheless, there are many aspects which do not represent the suspected historical truth. Still today there are members of the remaining Powhatan Nation. Their Chief, called Roy crazy horse, passed a comment regarding the Disney movie. He complained about the movie, trying to make Disney change the plot according to the history. However, his wish was refused due to the fact that Roy Disney responded that the film is "responsible, accurate, and respectful." (Chief Roy crazy horse). Pocahontas' tribesmen, however, criticize that the movie distorts the historical reality (cf. ibid.).

As already described in chapter four, Pocahontas was only the nickname of the girl Matoaka. Furthermore, it is shown that Pocahontas saved John Smith from being executed by her father. One the one side, this situation might have been an elaborate adoption ceremony since the Chief accepted Smith as a son. On the other side, Pocahontas would have only been about ten or eleven years old and not a young woman as shown in the movie. Therefore, it is conjectured that both did not have a romantic relationship. John Smith wrote about this heroic rescue seventeen years later, when Pocahontas had been already taken to England, peptized and famous. Yet, he used to write during his winter stay with Pocahontas' tribe, therefore, it is questioned why he did not mention her rescue earlier (cf. ibid.).

Additionally, Disney changed to whole ending of the story. Whereas Pocahontas in the movie decides to stay with her family and Smith returns to England to get medical treatment, the real Pocahontas was kidnapped and brought to England under duress when she was seventeen years old. Against the assumption that Pocahontas married John Rolfe for love, the Powhatan Nation even reproaches that she did it to be released from her captivity. After Pocahontas' death, the English around Smith and Rolfe fought against the Native Americans who had earlier helped and welcomed them. People were exterminated and lands were taken (cf. ibid.)

6. Racism and Stereotypes in Pocohontas (1995)

What can you expect

from filthy little heathens?

Their whole disgusting race is like a curse

Their skin's a hellish red

They're only good when dead

They're vermin, as I said

And worse.

They're savages! Savages!

Barely even human. Savages! Savages!

Drive them from our shore!

They're not like you and me

Which means they must be evil.

We must sound the drums of war!

(Taken from http://www.disneyclips.com/lyrics/lyrics69.html, retrieved 2015/08/12)

These are the lyrics of a song called "Savages, savages" taken from the Disney movie Pocahontas. Governor Ratcliff and his English crew sing it while they are preparing to fight
against the Indians. It is only one example of the racist language used in the movie.

In the second line, the Indians are called "filthy little heathens". Filthy can mean dirty
and also terrible, a quality that refers to the look but also to the character of a person. Being
dirty hints at not washing himself or herself or not being able to wear clean clothes. This impression is underlined by the following word "heathens". It can either refer to the religious
background where it is used from Christians to call people who do not have the Christian religion, but it can also mean that somebody is uncivilized. Both options seem to be meant offen-
sively and attack the Indian population.

The following line even surpasses the previous lines, because the English Governor
Ratcliff calls the Indians "disgusting", which is a clear symbol of his aversion towards them.
Furthermore, he sings that they are like a curse, which is the evil or the misfortune.

In line four, the Native American's skin is "hellish red", which again hints at the evil
coming from hell. This is underlined by the strong red skin-color all Indians have in Disney's
movie. Here we can find a stereotype of an Indian person. According to Fleming (2006),
many non-Native-American people think that they are easy to identify. Usually, there is the
stereotype of being dark or even red skinned, having high cheekbones and the black hair tied

16

up in braids. But there are also some blond Indians who have blue eyes or others who have features of African Americans (cf. ibid, p. 215). Disney, however, creates the image that all Native Americans have red skin, long black hair and dark eyes. Furthermore, there is the stereotype, created through Disney and other movies like Winnetou that all Indians wear Moccasins and a loincloth between their legs, although the real Pocahontas would have been naked during summer and would have worn fur in winter to warm herself (cf. Stebbins 2010).

"They're only good when dead" in line five shows the superiority that the English feel towards the Indians. Furthermore, they are called "vermin" which can either refer to toxic and objective animal collections that are difficult to control or to people that are obnoxious, both unpleasant and harmful.

The description "savages" underlines repeatedly this humiliation towards the Native American people and portrays them as wild, uncivilized and brutal. They are not like the English, which means that they must be evil and can therefore hardly be human. Here we can clearly see the form of Othering, since the British declare themselves as "normal" and the Indians as different. Moreover, the Governor sings that his crew should "[d]rive them from our shore". Although the land belonged to the Native Americans and the English settlers were the ones coming, it is self-evident for them that it now belongs to the British, who feel superior, and that the Indians must be killed. The whole song can therefore be seen as racist.

Already at the beginning of the film, when the crew is entering the ship *Susan Constant*, there is a dialogue between two crew members and John. One of them asks: "Are you coming on this voyage, too?". "Of course he is, you half-wit. You can't fight Indians without John Smith.", answers the other man. And John replies "That's right. I'm not about to let you boys have all the fun". In this scene, John Smith describes fighting against the Indians as being fun and does not want to miss this "amusement". He feels superior because he had fought against other tribes and had won.

This can also be seen in the following scene: John and Pocahontas have just met and slowly start to talk and to like each other. Pocahontas asks John where he comes from and wants to get information about his native country England. John responds that he is from London and that everything is different there. He mentions the carriages, streets and gigantic buildings which are high as trees. Pocahontas is fascinated and says that she would like to see everything. John explains to her that there will come the time when she will be able to see all this, because his crew came to build everything and to bring the progress to the New World.

John Smith:	[...] "We'll show your people how to use this land properly. How to make the most of it.".
Pocahontas:	"Make the most of it?"
John Smith:	"Yes, we'll build roads and decent houses and—
Pocahontas:	"Our houses are fine."
John Smith:	"You think that, only because you don't know any better [...] There's so much we can teach you. We've improved the lives of savages all over the world.
Pocahontas:	"Savages?!"
John Smith:	"Uh, not that you're a savage."
Pocahontas:	"Just my people."

In this conversation it becomes obvious again that John Smith sees Pocahontas and the other Native Americans as different. He, as a civilized, intelligent white man, wants to show the uncivilized Indians who are backward in development how to make the biggest profit out of their land. It can be clearly seen that the English are interested in forcing their standards and ideas of a good world on the Indians. At the same time, John depicts Pocahontas as naïve because he claims that she is confident with her housing situation since she does not know any better due to the fact that she has never seen a modern, English house. He moreover openly calls Pocahontas and her tribe savages, which offends her.

In the beginning of the movie, the English in general are portrayed as money-mad and profit-oriented. The reason why Governor Ratcliff and his crew come to the New World is because they want to find gold and become rich as it the Spanish did in other parts of the American continent. Although they steal the Indian's land and destroy their environment, the Governor sings a cheerful song called "Digging in Virginia", which plays the whole situation down. Moreover, the English are depicted as if they were only interested in their own success and development and constantly talk in an offending and aggressive way about the Indians, they call them e.g. throughout the whole movie (bloodthirsty) savages, to show that they are different and of lower status. Within the time, John Smith changes his mind through getting to know Pocahontas and falling in love with her. At the end, when he is supposed to be executed and Pocahontas throws herself between her love and her father, she can convince her father that war and fights are not the right way to treat each other and then the English take down their guns as well. When Governor Ratcliff, however, tries to shoot Powhatan dead but accidently hits John, all the English are against their commander and arrest him. This happy ending did not happen in real history since the English troops around John Smith and John Rolfe actually killed all the Indians and took over their land. Here we can see a belittlement of the real cruel and terrible procedure of the settlers. Furthermore, it is a slander that the English usually exterminated all Natives and did not accept them as shown in the movie. This can be seen as a loss of respect towards all American Indians, because their real historical happenings are not presented.

Finally, according to Chief Roy Crazy Horse (2013), Pocahontas is famous because she became the "good Indian" for Euro-Americans, the one who saved the life of a white man (cf. ibid.). Consequently, being a good or a bad Indian is a prominent theme in the movie. Naïve Americans are portrayed in a stereotypical way, because the audience learns that Indians are evil and bad and that there are only some exceptions such as Pocahontas.

7. Conclusion

The analysis of the Disney movie Pocahontas showed that there can be found various racists and stereotypical aspects. First of all, the ending of the film plays the cruelness of the English settlers down. In reality, the Indians were killed by the intruders and their lands were taken away. In Disney's movie, however, the audience can see a happy, joyful ending where Pocahontas saved Smith's love from death, achieved peace between the two groups and finally decides to stay with her tribe because she was needed. This is offending against the Native American population because their real and brutal sorrow is idealized and romanticized.

Moreover, the racism in the movie Pocahontas can be principally seen in the language the figures, above all the Governor Ratcliff and John Smith, use. Right from the beginning, the Native Americans are called savages, sometimes also depicted as bloodthirsty. When John and Pocahontas meet and he tells her about his developed home town London, he even calls her and her tribe savages and Pocahontas feels severely offended about it. Throughout the whole movie it is shown that the English settlers feel superior towards the Indians, primarily because of their equipment and their weapons. They think they are cleverer and have to show them how civilized and educated people are. The effect of Othering can be seen here clearly through that the English see themselves as normal and the Indians as different.

This is underlined by the lyrics of the film's music. When the English start to dig for gold and to take over the land, the cheerful song "Dig in Virginia", sang by the Governor Ratcliff, gives the impression that they would not do any harm to anyone. An even more offensive way of attacking the Indians is Governor Ratcliff's song "Savages, savages" where he calls them filthy, disgusting and that they are only good when they are dead. It is clear that Native American children and adults, who see this movie could feel bad and inferior.

Furthermore, the image of good and bad Indians is presented. As Chief Roy Crazy Horse claimed, Non-Native-Americans only remember Pocahontas because rescued the white John Smith from being executed. People could adopt the stereotype that there are only some good Indians and the rest is evil. In addition to that, the movie's audience sees a stereotype of a Native American, being red skinned and wearing leather clothes. According to Fleming (2006) it is important to underline that there is no typical Indian and that not everybody is dark or red skinned, has long brown hair but also blond or African American Indians.

To sum up it can be said that the movie does have racist elements and includes stereotypes. Nevertheless, it is a successful movie that deals with an important topic. Parents, as well as teachers should make children aware of the negative features and discuss them together.

8. Reference list

Printed Literature

Essed, P. (2000). Beyond antiracism: diversity, multi-identifications and sketchy images of new societies. In Reisigl, M. & R. Wodak (Ed.), Passagen Diskursforschung. *The semiotics of racism. Approaches in critical discourse analysis* (pp. 41–61). Wien: Passagen.

Fredrickson, G. M. (2002). *Racism: A short history.* Princeton, N.J: Princeton University Press.

Mossiker, F. (1976). *Pocahontas: The life and the legend* (1st ed). New York: Knopf; Distributed by Random House.

Sundquist, Å. (1987). *Pocahontas & co: The fictional American Indian women in nineteenth-century literature: a study of method.* Atlantic highlands (N. J.), Oslo: Humanities press international; Solum.

Online Literature

Abele, S. von (2005). *Human Migration Guide.* Retrieved August 14, 2015 from http://www.nationalgeographic.com/xpeditions/lessons/09/g68/migrationguidestudent.pdf.

Bernasconi, R. & T. L. Lott (2000). *The idea of race.* Hackett readings in philosophy. Indianapolis: Hackett Pub. Co. Retrieved August 14, 2015 from https://goo.gl/fxfkHf.

Bodenhausen, G. V. & J. A. Richeson (2010). *Prejudice, Stereotyping, and Discrimination.* In Baumeister, R. F. & Finkel, E. J. (Ed.), Advanced Social Psychology. The state of the Science (pp. 341–383). Oxford, New York: Oxford University Press. Retrieved August 14, 2015 from http://faculty.wcas.northwestern.edu/bodenhausen/BRAdvanced.pdf.

Boren, C. (2015). *Christian Taylor tweeted his fears after Michael Brown killing in Ferguson.* Retrieved August 14, 2015, from Washington Post: https://www.washingtonpost.com/news/early-lead/wp/2015/08/09/christian-taylor-tweets-on-police-killings-show-fears-founded-in-ferguson-killing/.

Brons, L. (2015). *Othering, an Analysis.* Transcience, 6(1), 69–90. Retrieved August 14, 2015 from http://www2.hu-berlin.de/transcience/Vol6_No1_2015_69_90.pdf.

Chief Roy Crazy Horse (2013). *The Pocahontas Myth.* Retrieved August 12, 2015, from http://www.powhatan.org/pocc.html.

Dovidio, J. F., Hewstone, M., Glick, P. & V. M. Esses (2010). Prejudice, Stereotyping and Prejudice, Stereotyping and Discrimination: Theoretical and Empirical Overview. In Dovidio, J. F., Hewstone, M., Glick, P. & V. M. Esses (Ed.), *The SAGE Handbook of Prejudice, Stereotyping and Discrimination* (pp. 3–29). London: SAGE Publications. Retrieved August 14, 2015 from http://www.sagepub.in/upm-data/54590_dovido,_chapter_1.pdf.

Erhart, R. (2013). *The Content of Native American Cultural Stereotypes in Comparison to Other Racial Groups.* Retrieved August 12, 2015, from http://hdl.handle.net/2286/R.A.110701.

Fleming, W. C. (2006). *Myths and Stereotypes About Native Americans*. Retrieved August 12, 2015, from http://webserv.jcu.edu/education/ed350/Myths%20and%20Stereotypes%20About%20Native%20Americans.pdf.

Fredrickson, G. M. (2003). *The Historical Origins and Development of Racism*. Retrieved August 13, 2015, from http://www.pbs.org/race/000_About/002_04-background-02-01.htm.

Kervyn, N., Fiske, S. T. & V. Y. Yzerbyt (2013). *Integrating The Stereotype Content Model (Warmth And Competence) And The Osgood Semantic Differential (Evaluation, Potency, And Activity)*. European journal of social psychology, 43(7), 673–681. Retrieved August 13, 2015, from http://www.fiskelab.org/storage/publications/Kervyn_2.pdf.

McGarty, C., Yzerbyt, V. Y. & R. Spears (2002). *Stereotypes as Explanations: The formation of meaningful beliefs about social groups*. Retrieved August 13, 2015, from Cambridge University Press: http://catdir.loc.gov/catdir/samples/cam033/2002073438.pdf.

Morenus, D.: *The Real Pocahontas*. Retrieved August 11, 2015, from http://pocahontas.morenus.org/.

Pigliucci, M. & J. Kaplan (2003). *On the Concept of Biological Race and Its Applicability to Humans*. Philosophy of Science, 70(5), 1161–1172. Retrieved August 11, 2015, from http://people.oregonstate.edu/~kaplanj/2003-PhilSc-race.pdf.

Rogers, D. & M. Bowman (2003). *A History: The Construction of Race and Racism: Dismantling Racism Project Western States Center*. Retrieved August 11, 2015, from http://www.racialequitytools.org/resourcefiles/Western%20States%20-%20Construction%20of%20Race.pdf.

Rountree, H. C.: *Pocahontas (d. 1617)*. Retrieved August 11, 2015, from http://www.encyclopediavirginia.org/Pocahontas_d_1617.

Staszak, J.-F. (2008). Other/otherness. In Thrift, N. J. & R. Kitchin (Eds.), *International encyclopedia of human geography* (pp. 43–47). Amsterdam, London, Oxford: Elsevier. Retrieved August 14, 2915, from http://goo.gl/qScIRN

Stebbins, S. J. (2010). *Pocahontas: Her Life and Legend*. Retrieved August 11, 2015, from http://www.nps.gov/jame/learn/historyculture/pocahontas-her-life-and-legend.htm.

9. Appendix

Picture 1: Engraved portrait of Native American Pocahontas of the Powhatan tribe circa 1610, she wears a shawl, feathered headdress, and European-styled necklace. Source:
http://img.timeinc.net/time/daily/2007/0705/360_james_pocahontas_0507.jpg, retrieved 2015/08/11

Picture 2: Smith Rescued by Pocahontas. Christian Inger, 1870. Imaginary Scene. Source:
http://www.encyclopediavirginia.org/media_player?mets_filename=evm00000019mets.xml, retrieved 2015/08/11

MARRIAGE OF POCAHONTAS & ROLFE.

Picture 3: Marriage of Virginia Indian Pocahontas and English colonist John Rolfe. Source:
http://www.encyclopediavirginia.org/media_player?mets_filename=evm00002810mets.xml, retrieved
2015/08/11

Picture 4: Baptism of Pocahontas. John Gadsby Chapman, 1837. Source:
http://www.encyclopediavirginia.org/media_player?mets_filename=evm00002822mets.xml,
retrieved 2015/08/11

Picture 5: Portrait of Pocahontas. Only image of
Pocahontas done from life. Source:
http://www.npg.org.uk/collections/search/portraitLar
ge/mw133760/Pocahontas?LinkID=mp55422&searc
h=sas&sText=pocahontas&role=sit&rNo=0, retrieved 2015/08/11

Picture 6: Portrait of Captain John Smith. Source:
http://www.kingsacademy.com/mhodges/04_American-
Government/01_Colonial-Foundations/pictures/John-
Smith.jpg, retrieved 2015/08/11

Picture 7: Pocahontas wears pearls and a European-style fashionable dress in this mid-nineteenth-century oil painting by Thomas Sully. Source: http://www.encyclopediavirginia.org/media_player?mets_filename=evm00000043mets.xml, retrieved 2015/08/11

YOUR KNOWLEDGE HAS VALUE

- We will publish your bachelor's and master's thesis, essays and papers

- Your own eBook and book - sold worldwide in all relevant shops

- Earn money with each sale

Upload your text at www.GRIN.com
and publish for free

Lightning Source UK Ltd.
Milton Keynes UK
UKHW011012161120
373487UK00002B/522